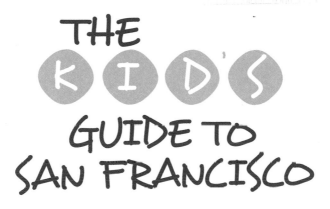

THE KID'S GUIDE TO SAN FRANCISCO

THE
KID'S

GUIDE TO
SAN FRANCISCO

1st
edition

Eileen Ogintz

Guilford, Connecticut
Helena, Montana
An imprint of Rowman & Littlefield

Globe Pequot is an imprint of Rowman & Littlefield

Distributed by NATIONAL BOOK NETWORK

Copyright © 2015 Eileen Ogintz

Illustrations licensed by Shutterstock.com

British Library Cataloguing-in-Publication Information available

Library of Congress Cataloging-in-Publication Data

Ogintz, Eileen.
  The kid's guide to San Francisco / Eileen Ogintz. — 1st edition.
     pages cm
  Includes index.
  ISBN 978-1-4930-0151-4 (pbk.)
  1. San Francisco (Calif.)—Guidebooks—Juvenile literature. 2. Children—Travel—California—San Francisco—Guidebooks. I. Title.
  F869.S33O37 2014
  917.94'610454—dc23

                                                          2014037114

∞™ The paper used in this publication meets the minimum requirements of American National Standard for Information Sciences—Permanence of Paper for Printed Library Materials, ANSI/NISO Z39.48-1992.

All the information in this guidebook is subject to change. We recommend that you call ahead to obtain current information before traveling.

Thank you to my daughter Regina Yemma and the students at the Children's Day School in San Francisco where she teaches for lending their insights. Santa Cruz teacher Tom Postlewaite and his students at the Santa Cruz Montessori Wavecrest Junior High told me what would be the most fun for kids in their area. Thanks also to San Francisco State University students Anne Liu and Carmen Chan who interviewed visiting and local kids in San Francisco and high school student Deanna Davidson who discerned kids' favorites at the Monterey Bay Aquarium. Thank you to Laurie Armstrong from the San Francisco Convention and Visitors Bureau for making sure I understood San Francisco and my daughter Melanie Yemma for fact-checking. Special thanks to all the visiting and local kids and parents who spent time talking to me about their experiences in and around the City by the Bay.

Contents

1
Welcome to the City by the Bay

PURE GOLD!

A few sparkles in the sand of a riverbed north of San Francisco changed this city forever.

Just 500 people lived here in 1847. But with the **1849 gold rush,** San Francisco became a big city almost overnight, bursting with people from all over the world who were coming and going from the goldfields. Fortunes were made and lost.

Now you know why San Francisco's professional football team is called the 49ers!

It was a wild and crazy place. One neighborhood, the Barbary Coast, was notorious for its lawlessness. Men outnumbered women there 10 to 1.

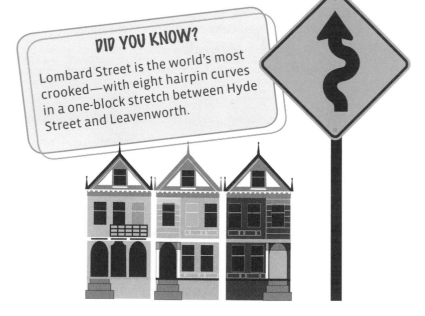

DID YOU KNOW?

Lombard Street is the world's most crooked—with eight hairpin curves in a one-block stretch between Hyde Street and Leavenworth.

Chinese, Japanese, Hispanic, African-American, Italian, Irish, and Filipino immigrants were among those who came here hoping to get rich. Many of their families have lived here ever since.

Ever since these gold rush days, San Francisco has been known as a place where new ideas flourish and differences between people are celebrated. Many artists, musicians, writers, and even chefs found their start here.

The hippie movement took off in the Haight neighborhood, and a lot of great rock 'n' roll was first played in San Francisco. A strong gay community developed here, and its fight against AIDS has been especially active.

DID YOU KNOW?

There are 14,000 Painted Lady Victorian houses in San Francisco. For many people, they represent San Francisco as much as the cable cars do.

{ **What's Cool?** The free Cable Car Museum where you can see how cable cars work (1201 Mason St.; 415-474-1887; cablecarmuseum.com).

There are great museums—whether you like art, science, or history—and great places to see theater and hear music. There are amazing parks and playgrounds including the city's biggest and most famous—Golden Gate Park.

Look at the city as you go up and down the hills—there are modern skyscrapers like the city's tallest, the Transamerica Pyramid downtown—853 feet high—and colorful Victorian houses called Painted Ladies.

Hike up to the top of **Telegraph Hill** for the views. San Francisco really looks different than other American cities. That's why it's so much fun to visit.

Hop off the **cable car** and check out Lombard Street, the most crooked street in the world. Does it make you dizzy?

A LOCAL KID SAYS:
"Cable cars are fun because you get to go up steep hills and go down them too."
—Louis, 10

DID YOU KNOW?

San Francisco is called "the City by the Bay" because it is at the very tip of a peninsula surrounded by water on three sides: the Pacific Ocean, San Francisco Bay, and the Golden Gate Strait, the narrow passage between them.

It's hard to believe that San Francisco was once a sleepy little town!

Look for the narrow stairways hidden in the gardens in nearby Russian Hill. (You'll find some steps on Greenwich between Hyde and Larkin.) This neighborhood of big old houses gets its name from when a small Russian cemetery was discovered at the top of the hill during the Gold Rush.

Got a cardboard box? The **Seward Street Slides** (Seward St. off Douglass St.) are really, really steep concrete slides. Fun!

Persistence Pays Off

On a drizzly night in 1869—more than 145 years ago—a young engineer watched horrified as a horse pulling a street-car up a steep San Francisco hill stumbled in the mud and fell and the crowded car rolled all the way back down.

Andrew Hallidie thought there had to be a better way to get people up and down San Francisco's hills. Even though many people laughed, he kept working on the idea to have an underground steel cable pull those cars.

He was right! The first cable car in the world, the Clay Street Hill Railroad, officially opened September 1, 1873, and was an immediate hit. Within a few years, San Francisco's cable cars were carrying people all over the city. Soon, there were cable railways in many cities across the country.

But only San Francisco's cable cars are still running. The shiny red cars of today look much like the originals that Hallidie designed. Stop at the **Cable Car Museum** (1201 Mason St.; 415-474-1887; cablecarmuseum.com) in the Cable Car Barn at Washington and Mason Streets on Nob Hill. It's where the cars are kept at night and also where you can look over the balcony and see the giant wheels turning, pulling the cables under San Francisco's streets. They're attached by a mechanical grip below the car. Climb aboard one of the old cars and see how it would feel to drive one!

Cable Car Smarts

Cable cars are different than buses or subways. Take the Powell-Hyde line if you want to go down the steepest hills. Here are some tips for happy riding:

- Cable cars stop at most corners along their routes. Look for the maroon-and-white cable car stop signs. Wave to alert the gripman to stop.

- Use either side to board but be careful of traffic.

- Don't stand in the space between the gripman and the front door. It must be kept clear. The same goes for floor spaces marked in yellow.

- Face the direction you're going. Don't lean out from the running boards and be sure to hold on around the curves.

- Tell the gripman or conductor when you want to get off.

A VISITING KID SAYS:
"You can get cool postcards of pictures from all around the city."
—Marcus, 11, Los Angeles, CA

The First Blue Jeans

Twenty-five-year-old Levi Strauss came to San Francisco in the middle of the gold rush, but he didn't make his fortune in the goldfields. Instead he invented the first blue jeans. May 20, 1873, is considered the birthday of blue jeans because that was the day that Levi Strauss and Jacob Davis obtained a US patent on the process of putting rivets in men's work pants for the very first time to keep pockets from tearing. They were called "waist overalls." Denim pants had been around as work wear for many years, but it was the act of placing rivets in these pants for the first time that created what we now call jeans. Today Levi Strauss & Co. is still headquartered in San Francisco. (levistrauss.com).

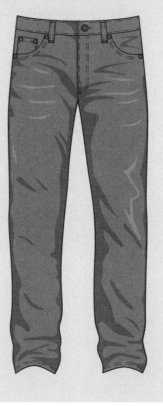

Earthquakes

Just after 5 a.m. on Wednesday, April 18, 1906, the first big shake jolted everyone out of bed. In those few moments, the city was changed forever. The **Virtual Museum of the City of San Francisco** (sfmuseum.org) can show you more about it. Huge buildings collapsed. Trees were uprooted. Entire houses were moved by the force of the initial quake and then the second that struck later that morning. People were running around the streets in their pajamas. Thousands died. Huge underground water mains broke all over town, and more than 50 fires erupted. Three-fourths of the city burned because the firefighters couldn't get the water to fight them. But a few hydrants kept working. Find the gold one on Church Street near Mission Dolores. The neighbors give it a fresh coat of paint every year because, the story goes, its water helped firefighters save the houses here. All across the city, the rebuilding started right away. The city came back bigger and better than ever. Look around. It still is.

DID YOU KNOW?

The 1906 earthquake didn't destroy the city. It was the fires afterward that did the damage. They burned for three days and nights.

TELL THE ADULTS:

There's a lot to do in and around San Francisco that's free—or nearly free:

Free museums include the **Randall Museum** (199 Museum Way; 415-554-9600; randallmuseum.org), **San Francisco Cable Car Museum** (1201 Mason St.; 415-474-1887; cablecarmuseum.com), and **Wells Fargo History Museum** (420 Montgomery St.; 415-396-2619; wellsfargohistory.com). Other museums are free at certain times.

Check out sf.funcheap.com for a calendar of free events.

The **Golden Gate Park Band** gives free Sunday afternoon concerts April through October on the Music Concourse (50 Hagiwara Tea Garden Dr.; 415-831-5500; sfrecpark.org).

There are free recitals at the **San Francisco Conservatory of Music** (50 Oak St.; 415-864-7326; sfcm .edu).

Free tours with the **San Francisco City Guides** include the Golden Gate Bridge and Chinatown (Polk Gulch; 415-557-4266; sfcityguides.org; a $5 donation is recommended).

Free tours in summer are given by Discover Walks of Chinatown, North Beach, and Fisherman's Wharf.

Walk or bike across the **Golden Gate Bridge** (415-921-5858; goldengatebridge.org).

Talk to the farmers at the **Ferry Building**'s huge farmers' market (1 Ferry Building; 415-291-3276; ferrybuildingmarketplace.com).

Check out a free Sunday class at the **Yerba Buena Gardens' Learning Gardens** (750 Howard St.; 415-820-3550; yerbabuenagardens.com).

Watch a Giants game for free at the **Knothole Gang**—the Giants right field wall with open archways where you can walk up and see the game without paying (24 Willie Mays Plaza, 415-972-2000; sfgiants.com).

Find a playground (sfrecpark.org has a list).

Have a picnic at the Marina Green or Crissy Field along the waterfront where the Golden Gate Bridge and Alcatraz are your backdrop (1199 E. Beach; 415-561-7690; presidio.gov).

Staying Safe on Vacation

- Write down the name and phone number of the hotel where you are staying. Also write down your parents' phone numbers—or make sure they are in your phone. Carry these numbers with you wherever you go.

- Practice "what-if" situations with your parents. What should you do if you get lost in a museum? A theme park? On a city street?

- Only ask uniformed people for help if you get lost— police officers, firefighters, store security guards, or museum officials wearing official badges.

- Wherever you go, decide on a central and easy-to-locate spot to meet in case you get separated.

A VISITING KID SAYS:
"Whenever I'm sightseeing, I always have my phone with me so I can take cool pictures and find my friends or parents if we get separated."
—Savannah, 13, Tiffin, OH

CONNECT THE DOTS

Connect the dots to draw the Golden Gate Bridge!

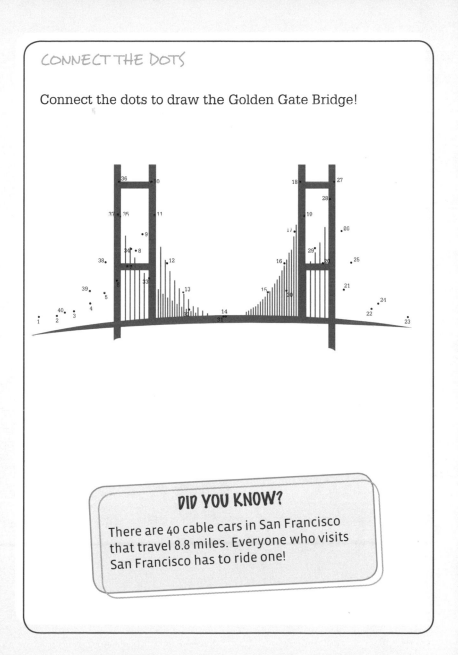

DID YOU KNOW?

There are 40 cable cars in San Francisco that travel 8.8 miles. Everyone who visits San Francisco has to ride one!

2

Towers & Hidden Gardens

GOT YOUR COMFIEST SHOES?

You're going to need them to explore San Francisco's neighborhoods. You'll miss a lot if you don't get out and walk, bike, or skateboard.

Some kids spend all their time in their own neighborhood, even though they live in a big city. Ask kids you meet to point out their favorite playground or place to get pizza or ice cream.

San Francisco is a lot more than its famous waterfront and big buildings. The hardest part is deciding which area of the city you want to explore first:

- **Union Square** is where all tourists go to shop. You might be staying here in a hotel. A lot of visitors to San Francisco do. You'll probably catch a cable car

A LOCAL KID SAYS:
"When I'm sightseeing, I like to have binoculars with me."
—Wes, 11

ride here. If you do, stop in at the San Francisco Visitor Center downstairs from the cable car terminus (900 Market St.; 415-391-2000; sanfrancisco.travel). They can answer all your questions—and give you discount coupons too.

- **Chinatown,** just a few blocks uphill from Union Square, is the oldest Chinese community in the country. It is bordered by Bush, Kearny, and Powell Streets.

DID YOU KNOW?
The Japanese have celebrated the arrival of the cherry blossoms every spring for more than 1,000 years.

吉 平 吉

What's Cool? The wild parrots you might see and hear squawking high in the trees on Telegraph Hill.

- **SOMA** is what the area "South of Market Street" is called. SOMA is home to lots of museums and the Yerba Buena Gardens, which have lots of great kids' activities.

- **Nob Hill** and **Russian Hill,** with their steep streets, cool houses and buildings, and hidden gardens, have awesome views! Check out the Ina Coolbrith Park carved from a steep hill (Vallejo Street between Mason and Taylor Streets).

A LOCAL KID SAYS:
"My favorite playground is at Mission Dolores Park."
—Andrea, 11

- **North Beach** is known for its famous Italian restaurants and old-fashioned bakeries, although more young people than Italians live here now. Walk down the Filbert Steps from the Coit Tower! If you are interested in writing, take a walk down Kerouac Alley (next to the famous City Lights Bookstore at 261 Columbus Ave.; citylights.com) to read quotes from famous writers like Lawrence Ferlinghetti, Jack Kerouac, and Maya Angelou.

- **The Richmond,** the neighborhood just north of Golden Gate Park, was once so far out of the city it was called Outer Lands, but today it's a big-city neighborhood with a small-town feel. It also has great views of the Golden Gate Bridge.

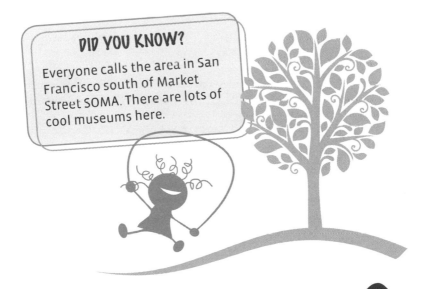

DID YOU KNOW?

Everyone calls the area in San Francisco south of Market Street SOMA. There are lots of cool museums here.

- **The Sunset** on the southern side of Golden Gate Park is home to the San Francisco Zoo. When you walk around here, it's hard to realize that there were sand dunes covering much of this area at one time.

- **The Haight** is where the hippie movement started, and **The Castro** is home to San Francisco's gay community.

- **The Mission** is where you'll find big colorful murals on the outside of buildings. Stop in at Mission Dolores Park where you're bound to meet some kids who live here playing at the playground—and their dogs!

Of course you won't get to all of San Francisco's neighborhoods. You might not even get to many of them. But you'll be missing a lot if you don't step off the regular tourist track and explore.

Just ask kids who live here!

DID YOU KNOW?

Lotta's Fountain was given to the city by Lotta Crabtree, a gold rush era actress, as a thank-you to her fans. It became a meeting place for people after the 1906 earthquake. Each April 18, the anniversary of the quake, people gather here at the intersection of Market Street, where Geary and Kearny Streets connect downtown.

Ditch the Car

How good are you at navigating?

San Francisco is a city to walk, bike, or get around like local kids and their parents—on public transportation. Not only is it easier, but you can congratulate yourself for traveling greener. Kids can get around on San Francisco's **Muni system**—buses, electric streetcars, and old-fashioned F-Line trolleys (sfmta.com).

You can get a one-day visitor's passport for $15 that gives you all the rides you want on Muni, including the cable cars, and multiday passes as well. Remember one cable car ride costs $6! Kids can ride on Muni buses for 75 cents—or free if they are younger than five. You can figure out your route on the website too!

San Francisco's subway is called **BART**—Bay Area Rapid Transit—and it is easy to use the one line through the city. It's good to take if you are going to the East Bay or San Francisco International Airport (bart.gov).

There are lots of places you can rent bikes and helmets such as **Blazing Saddles** (2715 Hyde St.; 415-202-8888; blazingsaddles.com) with several locations around the city and **Bay City Bike** (501 Bay St., Fisherman's Wharf; 415-346-BIKE).

Tell your parents you're ready to lead the way!

Festivals Are Made for Kids!

Whenever you visit, check to see if there is a special festival or fair. They've always got lots of fun things for kids to do:

JANUARY: Anniversary of the **Sea Lions' Arrival** at Pier 39 with special activities. (Check for dates at Beach Street and the Embarcadero; 415-981-7437; pier39.com.) Also the **Vietnamese Tet Festival** (Larkin Street; 415-351-1038; vietccsf.org) celebrates Vietnamese culture with a Tet Festival queen, food, music, colorful pageantry, and plenty of firecrackers in Little Saigon.

FEBRUARY: Chinese New Year lasts for nearly three weeks (chineseparade.com). Go to the Golden Dragon Parade!

MARCH: The **St. Patrick's Day Parade** takes place the Saturday closest to March 17 (2nd and Market to Civic Center; 415-395-8417; uissf.org). This is one of San Francisco's biggest parades! There is also the **Cherry Blossom Festival** in Japantown (Civic Center and Japantown; 415-563-2313; nccbf.org) with crafts, performances, martial arts, and a big parade.

MAY: Visit the **Cinco de Mayo Festival** on the Sunday nearest to May 5 in the Mission District for special kids' activities (Mission Dolores Park, Dolores Street between 18th and 20th Streets; mncsf.org). Bring a picnic and dance in the streets!

JUNE: The **Juneteenth Celebration** (Fillmore District between Geary and Eddy Streets; sfjuneteenth.org) celebrates the date that black Americans in Texas first learned of the end of slavery and the Civil War in Galveston, Texas, in 1865—two and a half years after Lincoln's Emancipation Proclamation.

JULY: Fireworks, local bands, food, and arts and crafts light up the annual **Fourth of July Waterfront Festival** (pier39.com).

SEPTEMBER: The **San Francisco Shakespeare Festival** holds outdoor performances on September weekends (sfshakes.org).

OCTOBER: The **LEAP Sandcastle Contest** (Ocean Beach, Great Highway; leaparts.org) brings together architects, engineers, contractors, designers, and San Francisco schoolchildren to collaborate every year in creating majestic sculptures from sand.

DECEMBER: Towering lighted trees help you get in the holiday spirit on the waterfront (Pier 39 and all four towers of the Embarcadero Center to Union Square and the Path of Gold streetlights on Market Street). The city's cable cars are festively decorated too and are available for holiday lights tours (classiccablecar.com).

TELL THE ADULTS:

Touring cities isn't only about famous sites and museums—especially in San Francisco. Leave a lot of time to explore the city's neighborhoods, play soccer in the park, go to a baseball or basketball game, or just take a ride on a cable car or trolley. You'll find the real San Francisco in neighborhoods where families like yours live, in playgrounds and parks. Most important, get the kids involved in the planning:

Let them help plan the itinerary starting at the official **San Francisco tourism website** (sanfrancisco.travel).

Bay Area Parent (bayareaparent.com) has a list of current kid-friendly events.

Check out local websites like sfgate.com/sfguide and sfstation.com for listings of events and 7x7.com for the locals' take on good eats, shopping, and more.

Take a virtual tour of museums and tourist sites before you visit and decide where you want to focus your attention. If you plan to go to many of the city's major museums and attractions, consider getting a **San Francisco CityPASS** (citypass.com/SanFrancisco), which will save you significant money on admissions and also allow you to bypass some of the lines.

If the kids are old enough, encourage each to plan a day or half day of your visit. At the very least, make sure each person in the family has a say in the itinerary.

Let the kids choose what they want to see at TIX Bay Area (415-433-7827; tixbayarea.com) where you can get half-price day-of seats to **concerts and plays** (at Union Square at Powell, Stocken Post and Geary Streets).

Plan plenty of downtime so you can enjoy San Francisco's parks, especially Golden Gate Park and the Presidio. You'll meet lots of local families there!

Giving Back to Firefighters

On her way home from school one day, Lillie Coit, who grew up during the gold rush, helped San Francisco firefighters douse a blaze. From then on, she made friends with firemen, playing cards with them and even wearing an honorary firefighter's uniform long before women were firefighters—or even wore pants.

There's a famous statue in Washington Square of two firefighters rescuing a young girl. It was donated by Lillie Coit.

After she died, she left money for the city to build a monument to honor firefighters. You can see that monument today—it's the 210-foot **Coit Tower** on top of Telegraph Hill. Stop and see the famous murals inside about what California life once was like. When Coit Tower is open, ride the elevator to the top. Some people think it looks like the nozzle of a fire hose!

DID YOU KNOW?

Grant Street is San Francisco's oldest street—it's been around since 1821.

Mission Street is the longest street in San Francisco at 7.29 miles!

FILL IN THE MISSING LETTERS IN THE NAMES OF
SOME SAN FRANCISCO NEIGHBORHOODS!

U NI O N S Q UAR E

C H IN A TOW N

S O M A

NO B HI L L

R US S IA N HI L L

NO R TH B E AC H

T H E RI C H M ON D

T HE SU N S E T

TH E H A IGH T

THE M ISSI O N

See page 148 for the answers
Fisherman's Wharf

{ **What's Cool?** Breakfast at the famous **Tartine Bakery** (600 Guerrero St.;
415-487-2600; tartinebakery.com) for its scrumptious pastries, breads, and
quiches, baked fresh every morning.

3
Sea Lions, Hyde Park &
Alcatraz Island

SEA LIONS OR SHARKS? SOUVENIRS OR HISTORIC SHIPS?

Maybe you just want to head to Pier 39 to see the famous resident sea lions play—and then go play yourself in the waterfront park.

The hardest part about **Fisherman's Wharf** is deciding where to go first.

You'll see everything here from historic boats at the Hyde Park Pier to street performers drawing cartoons or singing and playing instruments, shops selling every kind of souvenir, and stands selling seafood. You can pose with rock stars—actually wax figures that look real—at **Madame Tussauds** (145 Jefferson St.; madame tussauds.com/SanFrancisco), or if you dare, visit the **San Francisco Dungeon** (145 Jefferson St.; thedungeons.com/sanfrancisco).

DID YOU KNOW?

It takes nearly 1,000 pounds of food every week to feed all the animals that live at the Aquarium of the Bay (the Embarcadero and Beach Street; 415-623-5300; aquariumofthebay.org).

Have you ever tried Dungeness crab? It's a San Francisco specialty. No worries if you get hungry—you'll find every kind of **food** here from seafood to burgers and pizza. Head to Ghirardelli Square for dessert at Kara's Cupcakes or the Ghirardelli Soda Fountain and Chocolate Shop (900 North Point St.; 415-775-5500; ghirardellisq .com).

A VISITING KID SAYS:
"Don't miss the touch pools at the Aquarium of the Bay. We got to get up close and touch sharks, rays, and sea stars."
—Ethan, 11, Golden, CO

No wonder this is a busy place from morning until night!

After you've greeted the **sea lions** (they're at K Dock, West Marina), stop in at the Sea Lion Center to learn more about them (the Embarcadero at Beach St.; 415-262-4734; sealioncenter.org). Go for a ride on Pier 39's antique 2-level Venetian carousel or try the famous musical stairs—you make music whenever you walk up or down (pier39.com)!

There's a giant **arcade,** Magowan's Infinite Mirror Maze, and the San Francisco Magic Show at the Bay Theater right next to the Aquarium of the Bay here (Beach Street and the Embarcadero; 415-814-9521).

Watch the mimes, jugglers, and other street performers. Try the **7D Experience** (think a roller coaster and laser blasting game all rolled together) or **Frequent Flyers**—a bungee trampoline that's safe for kids. You can go 20 feet in the air.

At Pier 39 you could shop until your mom and dad drop, with so many stores selling everything from cable car T-shirts to plush sea lions to kites and posters of the Golden Gate Bridge.

What's Cool? Heading to Pier 45 on Fisherman's Wharf early in the morning to watch the anglers bring in their catch.

When you get tired, grab a snack and head to the 5-acre Waterfront Park or the Aquatic Park to play in the sand.

There are plenty of non-fishy attractions along Fisherman's Wharf too. There's the **Ripley's Believe It or Not Museum** (175 Jefferson St.; 415-202-9850; ripleys.com/san francisco) and an arcade like none you've ever seen: the **Musee Mecanique** with all kinds of old-fashioned arcades machines and mechanically operated instruments (Pier 45 Shed A; 415-346-2000; museemecanique.com). The owner started this collection when he was a kid, and it's been growing ever since.

Don't forget some quarters to play the games!

DID YOU KNOW?

You can take a ferry right from Fisherman's Wharf to Angel Island State Park in San Francisco Bay for a picnic, a bike ride, or to hunt for treasures on the beach (415-435-3544; angelisland.com).

Join the Sea Lion Party

They dive and fight, bark, and chase seagulls. When they get tired, they stretch out on the floating docks of the harbor to catch some sun. There are hundreds of sea lions who have made Pier 39 on San Francisco's Fisherman's Wharf their home.

They arrived shortly after the 1989 earthquake, and as soon as they discovered there were so many herring to eat in the water, they decided to stay and invited their friends to the never-ending party. You won't believe it till you see it.

On weekends, look for the **Marine Mammal Center** (marinemammalcenter.org) volunteers. They help rescue stranded and hurt sea lions and can tell you lots about them.

Sea lions may look like fish, but they're more like humans because they're mammals and require air to live.

Can you balance a ball on your nose? Sea lions can!

A LOCAL KID SAYS:
"The sea lions are very funny, especially the noise they make!"
—Hanna, 12

Eye to Eye with a Shark

Ready to get eye to eye with a seven-gill shark? They're the largest predator in San Francisco Bay! You can see them at the **Aquarium of the Bay** on Fisherman's Wharf Pier 39 (the Embarcadero and Beach Street; 415-623-5300; aquariumofthe bay.org).

Maybe you'd rather check out the moon jellies that were all born and raised here or touch a bat ray's wing. Walk through a clear tunnel while San Francisco Bay's animals swim overhead. Make sure not to miss the touch tanks!

Over 20,000 animals from San Francisco Bay and the nearby waters live here, and this is the place to learn all about them whether you walk under them, reach out and touch them, or just watch them in their tanks. You can see them get fed or sign up for a behind-the-scenes tour to learn more about how the naturalists care for them.

Check out the giant Pacific octopus. His eight arms are so strong, he can move more than 700 pounds!

What You Eat Can Help Save Sea Creatures!

Did you know that where you get the fish you eat directly impacts the health of sea creatures in the ocean? That's because their marine "home" is under intense pressure from overfishing and environmentally destructive fishing methods.

Seafood retailers and restaurants play a crucial role in the conservation of ocean resources because of where and how they get their fish—and so do you. When you support ocean-friendly seafood (called "sustainable seafood"), you help make change happen.

The Aquarium of the Bay, the California Academy of Sciences, and the San Francisco Zoo all work together on the **San Francisco Seafood Watch Alliance** (seafoodwatch.org). Here's how they say you can help:

- Go to restaurants that have pledged to serve sustainable seafood.

- Download the pocket guide that tells you what fish you should be ordering and eating in California (seafoodwatch .org/cr).

- Tell your friends!

Alcatraz

It's a small, rocky island just over a mile from Pier 33 at Fisherman's Wharf that was the site of the first lighthouse and US-built fort on the West Coast before it became *the* prison where no one wanted to end up.

Prisoners were sent to **Alcatraz Federal Penitentiary** (nps.gov/alca) because they wouldn't follow the rules at other prisons.

See what you think of Alcatraz when you take the ferry from Fisherman's Wharf. Be sure to buy your tickets in advance (alcatrazcruises.com or 415-981-7625)! There are evening tours too.

Because it is now a national park, US park rangers are here and can answer your questions. Walk down "Broadway," the busiest hallway in the cell house and step inside the narrow, bare blocks where the prisoners lived. Look at the dark, windowless cells dubbed "The Hole," where prisoners were sent for punishment. Their meals were served through a slot in the door. Walk around their exercise yard.

Think about the kids of the prison guards who lived on the island, taking the ferry to school every day.

Alcatraz was a federal prison for less than 30 years, until 1963. More than 100 cannons were brought here, but no one ever fired a shot in defense of the Bay.

Time Travel Aboard Ship

Ready to come aboard? The square-rigged **Balclutha** from the 1880s was typical of hundreds of ships that sailed from San Francisco to Europe carrying cargo—and news of the gold rush. Schoolkids come here for overnight field trips to see what it would have been like to be a sailor then. A park ranger can give you a tour. That's because the *Balclutha* at Hyde Park Pier is part of the San Francisco Maritime National Historical Park (499 Jefferson St.; 415-447-5000; nps.gov/safr).

The 1891 schooner **Alma** still goes out in the Bay. If you're lucky, you can join the adventure. Check out the **Thayer**, a lumber schooner that sailed from the Pacific Northwest down the California coast around the turn of the 20th century.

Don't miss the paddle steamboat ferry **Eureka,** the largest passenger ferry of her day, with all of her vintage cars. People rode ferries like the *Eureka* across San Francisco Bay before the Golden Gate and Bay Bridges were built.

Not far away is the **SS Jeremiah O'Brien** (ssjeremiahobrien .org). She's the last survivor of the World War II Liberty ships that ferried troops and supplies around the world.

Join the Celebration!

There are special festivals and activities all year long at **Pier 39** (Beach Street and the Embarcadero; 415-981-7437; pier39 .com). Check if these are going on when you visit:

- **JANUARY:** The anniversary of the sea lion's arrival is cause for a celebration.

- **FEBRUARY: Tulipmania** (Feb. 15) finds Pier 39 transformed into a bayside flower wonderland.

- **MARCH: Sunday Streets** allows kids of all ages to test their speed and agility on a gigantic obstacle course, learn about the sea lions, and taste local treats.

- **JULY:** Pier 39's **Fourth of July Celebration** pumps up the fun for the entire family.

- **OCTOBER:** Pier 39's **October Fireworks series** every Saturday in October brings live music and Pier 39's **Fleet Week Celebration** with a parade of ships, ship tours, and military band performances.

- **NOVEMBER:** Pier 39's **Tree Lighting Celebration** features a special holiday music sing-along for the whole family.

Fisherman's Wharf is packed with souvenir shops—and temptation that may be hard to resist. That's why it's smart to have a souvenir strategy before your trip. Here's how:

Discuss their souvenir budget. How much do you plan to give them for the trip? Do they have birthday money? An allowance? Earning from chores?

Store loose change in a big jar that the kids can use for souvenir spending.

Surprise them later on their birthday or at the holidays with something they wanted to buy in San Francisco but didn't think you'd purchased.

Steer them to souvenirs that will help them remember their trip to San Francisco, whether that means a stuffed sea lion, a toy cable car, or a San Francisco key chain, photo frame (for their favorite vacation picture), T-shirt, or hoodie. Or let them each choose a special Christmas tree ornament.

Encourage them to start a collection on the trip— postcards, pins, patches for their backpack, or stickers for their water bottle or laptop.

Discourage impulse buys.

A VISITING KID SAYS:
"We went on a boat cruise from Fisherman's Wharf that went under the Golden Gate Bridge."
—Sara, 12 Seattle, WA

Using the key, write the letters under the symbols to figure out the secret phrase.

For example: 🚲 🗺 🚇 ✈ = b i r d

_ _ _ _ _ _ _ _ _ _ _   _ _ _ _ _

a= ✔   b= 🚲   c= 🏙   d= ✈   e= 🎁

f= 🏭   g= 🏛   h= 🏡   i= 🚩   j= 🏚

k= 🌶   l= ?   m= !   n= 👁   o= 🚤

p= 🌲   q= ⛰   r= 🚇   s= ✦   t= 🗺

u= 📢   v= 📦   w= 🚩   x= 🔈   y= ♥

z= 💐   .= ◼   != 🚌   '= 🌶

See page 148 for the answers

Now try and make your own secret messages in the space below.

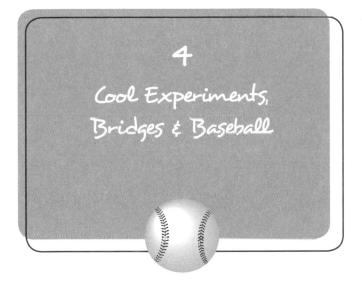

4

Cool Experiments, Bridges & Baseball

HOW GOOD IS YOUR POKER FACE?

You can find out at the **Exploratorium,** which is like no other museum you've ever seen. It's the world leader in learning outside of school. You'll have so much fun pushing buttons, turning cranks, and getting a close-up view of the critters that live in the water underneath the museum (Exploratorium Pier 15; 415-528-4420; exploratorium.edu).

And that's just the beginning. There's a big free outdoor space around the pier with outdoor exhibits as well as restaurants and food carts.

There are some 650 indoor and outdoor exhibits here in six main galleries. A lot of kids visit on field trips, and most families who travel to San Francisco come too.

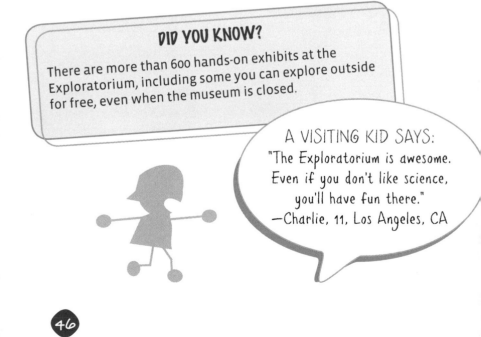

DID YOU KNOW?

There are more than 600 hands-on exhibits at the Exploratorium, including some you can explore outside for free, even when the museum is closed.

A VISITING KID SAYS:
"The Exploratorium is awesome. Even if you don't like science, you'll have fun there."
—Charlie, 11, Los Angeles, CA

It all began more than 45 years ago when a physicist and science teacher named Frank Oppenheimer decided he wanted to transform science education by making it hands-on and fun. Good idea, don't you think!

Ever since, Exploratorium scientists, builders, and teachers have pioneered ways to make science more engaging while helping you to understand scientific research and how it matters in your life. There are exhibits that explore biology, physics, how we see and listen, and how we behave—all interactive, of course.

There's a new center that considers how to use art to investigate the world—which means you'll see big temporary artworks outside and special exhibitions in the museum's Black Box.

{ **What's Cool?** Putting yourself in the cab at the "controls" of an old-fashioned streetcar at the San Francisco Railway Museum across from the Ferry Building (77 Steuart St.; 415-974 1948; streetcar.org).

Teens are part of the staff here. Look for "explainers" around the museum at the exhibits.

Kids love the **Tinkering Studio** where you can invent your own experiment—and then build it. One person turned a huge pegboard into the world's largest marble machine! Make sure to check out the **giant toothpick sculpture** just outside. How many famous San Francisco sites do you recognize in the toothpicks?

Another favorite is dancing and spinning with a column of fog at **Tornado.**

At Sound Bite, discover how you don't really need your ears to listen—not if you use your jawbone like a snake. Find out how we can't always believe what we see—white may really be black at **Bright Black.**

The East Gallery Living Systems is a working lab studying life that lives in the bay waters.

DID YOU KNOW?

San Francisco has 229 parks and playgrounds including the Brannan Street Wharf on the Embarcadero where, besides playing, you can learn all about the tides.

There's a 3D map of the Bay Area that shows what shapes this landscape, from fogs to earthquakes while the **Wired Pier** streams real-time data about the environment here—everything from the quality of the air and water to tides and pollution—to the Fisher Bay Observatory Gallery.

Have an idea for a new exhibit? There's an "exhibit making" workshop where you can see how museum staff create and build the exhibits on display—and watch them work. But these exhibits are never really done. They're always changing and getting better—just like you!

A LOCAL KID SAYS:
"My favorite thing at the Exploratorium is the mirror game. I can see myself many times!"
—William, 11

Water Smarts

The changing climate has been impacting water supplies with a prolonged drought in California. None of us can afford to waste water, especially here. The Exploratorium in San Francisco saves 60 percent of water usage by harvesting rainwater and having water-efficient plumbing throughout the building. Here's how you can help:

- Turn off the water when you brush your teeth.

- Take shorter showers and only fill the tub halfway when you take a bath.

- Don't use the toilet as a wastebasket (each flush uses 1.6 gallons of water!).

- Garden with plants that don't need a lot of water ... or grow food, not lawns.

A LOCAL KID SAYS:
"You shouldn't leave San Francisco without getting a Giants hat!"
—Wes, 11

Play Ball!

Check out the boats—from the baseball park! That's because AT&T Park, where the San Francisco Giants play, overlooks San Francisco Bay at South Beach Harbor. Some people even try to catch home-run balls from boats!

Kids love **AT&T Park** (24 Willie Mays Plaza; 415-972-2000; sanfrancisco.giants.mlb .com) because of the playground within the ballpark and Little Giants park where kids can hold their own game. Check out one of the world's largest baseball gloves. Did you notice it only has four fingers?

Parents love that, on the morning of the game, you might be able to get tickets for as little as $5 and you can bring your own picnic.

But this is one park where you can watch the game without paying anything. Just look for the **Knothole Gang** in the Giants right field wall and watch for free!

DID YOU KNOW?

One important difference between a fastball, curveball, or slider and a screwball is the direction in which the ball spins.

Talk to the Farmers

Have you ever seen a cranberry bean? Look around at all the kinds of apples!

There are farmers' markets all over San Francisco, but the **Ferry Building Farmer's Market** (1 Ferry Building; 415-693-0996; ferrybuildingmarketplace.com, cuesa.org) on San Francisco's wharf outside the Ferry Building on the Embarcadero is the most famous. It's held just certain days of the week, though you'll also find plenty of good eats inside the Ferry Building too.

Come to get fixings for a picnic. There are samples everywhere—apples, dried fruit, nuts, delectable chocolate. (How about chocolate almond brittle?)

This is a California Certified Farmers' Market, which means you have to be a farmer or a member of a farmer's family to sell your produce here. The farmers will be glad to talk to you about

DID YOU KNOW?

There are more than 200 kinds of stone fruits like peaches and plums sold at the Ferry Building Farmer's Market in summer (1 Ferry Building; 415-693-0996; ferrybuildingmarketplace.com).

what they grow, how their produce goes from their farm to the grocery store, and why you should eat vegetables and fruit that are in season. The number one reason: They taste better!

San Francisco's Ferry Building was where dozens of ferries arrived and left, carrying passengers and their cars across the Bay before the Golden Gate and Bay Bridges were constructed.

Today you'll find all kinds of delicious local eats—Acme bread, classic Italian gelato, and **Cowgirl Creamery cheese** (cowgirlcreamery.com), among other goodies. There are samples here too. This is the place to taste freshly made Mexican tamales and salsas, Vietnamese soup, and Chinese tea.

There's even **Far West Fungi** (farwestfungi.com) devoted to mushrooms and Hog Island Oyster Company.

Have you ever tried a raw oyster?

TELL THE ADULTS:

When you're in San Francisco, you've got to get out on the water! Some of the best views of the city are from the Bay and there are plenty of different options:

Take a cruise that will go beneath the Golden Gate Bridge. Options include the **Red & White Fleet** (from Pier 43½ on Fisherman's Wharf; 415-673-2900; redandwhite.com) and the **Blue & Gold Fleet** (Pier 41; 415-705-8200; blueandgoldfleet.com), which also offers the high-speed **RocketBoat** trips from May to October.

Sail away in a catamaran with **San Francisco Sailing Company** (Pier 39; 415-378-4887; sfsail.com) or, June to November, on the historic schooner *Alma* (Hyde Street Pier; 415-447-5000; nps.gov/safr).

Explore by kayak with a guide from **City Kayak** (South Beach Harbor; 415-294-1050; citykayak.com).

Take a ferry to explore across the bay to **Oakland, Sausalito,** or **Angel Island** (Pier 41; 415-773-1188; blueandgoldfleet.com).

Go whale watching with a company like **San Francisco Bay Whale Watching** out to the national marine sanctuary at the Farallon Islands (Pier 39, Beach and Embarcadero Streets; 415-331-6267; sfbaywhalewatching.com).

Go amphibious on **Ride the Ducks**, which offers a land and water tour on the same vehicle (2766 Taylor St.; 877-887-8225; sanfrancisco.ridetheducks.com).

Ah-Hah!

Have you ever thought about the color of water?

See how San Francisco Bay changes color by matching color swatches suspended above the water at the Exploratorium.

Outside the Exploratorium you'll see a large-scale temporary public art project called *Over the Water* and other **AH-HAH! exhibits** that are designed so you can observe and engage in the environment here like never before.

Check out the **Wave Organ** at the end of the breakwater. Its sounds are activated by waves and respond to the wind.

Experience your own rainstorm at **Remote Rains** by adjusting the size and frequency of raindrops.

Walk across the **Fog Bridge** that literally envelops you in fog and mist while the **Camera Obscura Cart** invites you to view the landscape and people passing by—upside down.

Spin disks filled with mud, sand, and gravel gathered at San Francisco Bay at **Bay Windows** and see the color created.

Don't miss **DAYLAY**—a sound and light installation in the pier above the water. Microphones record sound during the day and then play them back at night as LED lights reflecting off the water grow brighter and brighter.

What's your favorite AH-HAH moment here?

USE THE SPACE BELOW TO DRAW PICTURES OF
WHAT YOU SAW TODAY!

{ **What's Cool?** Navigating only by touch in the Exploratorium's pitch-black Tactile Dome.

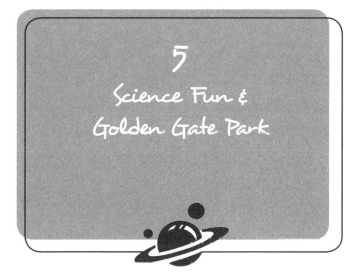

5
Science Fun &
Golden Gate Park

WEIRD & CRAZY CREATURES

Dive into the world's deepest living coral reef tank—without a wet suit.

Step inside a living rain forest complete with croaking frogs, butterflies, and chirping birds—without leaving San Francisco.

Take a look at the swamp where alligators rule or explore what it takes to live underwater in the California Coast exhibit.

Get up close and personal with penguins.

Compare fossils of our ancient human relatives. Did you know humans almost became extinct at one point?

Welcome to the **California Academy of Sciences** (55 Music Concourse Dr., Golden Gate Park; 415-379-8000; calacademy.org). It's home to an aquarium, planetarium, natural history museum, and 4-story rain forest—all under

DID YOU KNOW?

You can ride pigs and cats as well as horses on the old-fashioned carousel in Koret Children's Quarter.

one living roof in Golden Gate Park. Don't forget this is a major research institution too, studying one of the most important subjects of our time—the natural world and how we can help sustain it. The Science in Action exhibit displays the latest scientific discoveries daily. The academy's scientists identified 91 new plant and animal species—just in one year!

See remote islands like Madagascar and the Galapagos through their eyes and you'll understand how these far-flung places are laboratories for studying evolution. Examine the specimens they've collected and see how you'd do—ready to set a trap for a beetle? (Virtual, of course!)

No wonder kids and their parents flock here, whether they live in San Francisco or are visiting. If you ever thought science was boring, think again. There are tens of thousands of creatures here and hands-on activities throughout this big museum, even a **Discovery Tidepool.** (Have you ever held a sea star?)

Check out the **Living Roof** and see how it not only provides insulation and reduces heat but also creates a new habitat for native birds, butterflies, and other insects. See how the seven hills of the living roof are like San Francisco's hills?

Stand on the glass "bridge" and watch the sharks swim beneath you. See how many colors of fish you can count in the huge **Coral Reef Tank.** There are more than 2,000 of them.

Everyone loves exploring **The Rainforest of the World,** circling up a ramp through a glass dome that's 90 feet high. You'll see the amazing creatures that call

{ **WHAT'S COOL?** The 3-story rain forest at the California Academy of Sciences.

different rain forests home—piranhas from the Amazon, flying lizards from Borneo, bright green geckos from Madagascar.

You've got to love the **African penguins** too. They're part of a special program aimed at conserving this species in the wild because they are at high risk of becoming extinct.

A LOCAL KID SAYS:
"The de Young Museum is my favorite art museum in San Francisco. I like to look at the art and to shop at the store."
—Sara, 17

But this is also a terrific place to learn about the creatures that live along the California coast. One big tank recreates the marine habitats of the Gulf of the Farallones National Marine Sanctuary right near San Francisco.

Can you smell the seawater?

DID YOU KNOW?

Fortune cookies were invented in San Francisco but not in Chinatown. They were first served at the Japanese Tea Garden in Golden Gate Park (75 Hagiwara Tea Garden Dr.; 415-752-1171; japaneseteagardensf.com).

Flower Power!

Golden Gate Park is one place you've got to stop and smell the flowers—or at least look at them.

They're so pretty! Check out the giant greenhouse at the **Conservatory of Flowers** (100 John F. Kennedy Dr.; 415-831-2090; conservatoryofflowers.org). Look at the impressive 14-ton glass dome. It was shipped in pieces from England more than 135 years ago and then put back together.

Have you ever seen a plant eating bugs? You will here. If you come in summer or fall, you'll see the Dahlia Garden in bloom. And who knew there were so many kinds of rhododendron—there are 850 here at the Rhododendron Dell!

You'll see plants from places around the world with climates similar to San Francisco at the **San Francisco Botanical Garden** (1199 9th Ave.; 415-661-1316; sfbotanical garden.org). Kids really like the dwarf plants here.

You'll likely see flowers whenever you come—rhododendrons starting in February; the Queen Wilhelmina Tulip Garden that blooms in February and March, complete with a windmill; cherry blossoms in spring at the Japanese Tea Garden (don't miss the giant Buddha!), and the Rose Garden in the summer.

There's even an entire garden with all the plants mentioned in Shakespeare's plays.

What's your favorite?

Get Creative!

It's easy at the **de Young Museum** (50 Hagiwara Tea Garden Dr.; 415-750-3600; deyoung.famsf.org) in Golden Gate Park and at the **Asian Art Museum** (200 Larkin St.; 415-581-3500; asianart.org) whether you want to see the art or create it yourself. Both museums are free for kids 12 and under!

When you go to the de Young, look at the building before you even look at the art. A lot of people think it's strange. What do you think?

You have your pick of art to see here—it's from all over the world—but make sure not to miss the American and British paintings. The museum is famous for those collections.

Did you know the Asian Art Museum has the largest such collection outside Asia—going back 6,000 years? This is a great place to learn about the culture in Asia through its art. Whenever you visit:

- Stand in front of the art and pose like the people, animals, and shapes in the art.

- Make up a story about what you see.

- Imagine what you would hear, or smell, if you were inside the artwork.

Get Ready to Play!

Golden Gate Park is one huge park! There are 1,017 acres of trees, grass, hiking paths and bike trails, baseball diamonds and basketball courts, a golf course and tennis courts, playgrounds and ponds, places to watch outdoor concerts, and kid-friendly museums too.

- Rent skates or a bike; take a kite too!

- Take along a fishing pole and you can practice casting in front of Anglers Lodge.

- Take out a rowboat or paddleboat at Stow Lake. Or watch people sail their model boats on Spreckels Lake. You can too if you bring one!

- On Sunday, you might be able to hear the **Golden Gate Park Band** play. The concerts are free (goldengateparkband.org).

It's hard to remember that this whole place was once a huge sand dune that people called the Great Sand Wastes. Most didn't think a park could ever be built here.

Aren't you glad they were wrong?

Earthquake Smarts

Get ready for a big jolt! That's what being in an earthquake feels like. You can experience that feeling in the **earthquake simulator** at the California Academy of Sciences Earthquake exhibit. Learn how people in California and elsewhere around the world prepare for and respond to earthquakes, and explore the science of earthquakes and the impact of the biggest disaster in San Francisco history—the 1906 earthquake.

No one knows when—or where—the next major quake might strike. If you're in an earthquake, the experts say:

- Get under a strong piece of furniture, like a bed.

- Don't run outdoors. Stay away from windows.

- Don't get on an elevator. Use the stairs if you have to leave a building.

- If you're in a car, ask the driver to pull over. Watch for falling trees and wires.

DID YOU KNOW?

An earthquake's epicenter is the point on the ground where the greatest movement occurs. A seismograph is the instrument that records the earth's tremors and shows an earthquake's size. You'll find out more about earthquakes at the California Academy of Sciences.

TELL THE ADULTS:

Before visiting a big science center like the California Academy of Sciences (calacademy.org) or an art museum like the de Young Museum (deyoung.famsf .org/visit) or the Asian Art Museum (asianart.org), take a **virtual tour** with the kids to orient yourselves and figure out what you want to see most. That's a good idea too when visiting such a vast place as **Golden Gate Park** (sfrecpark.org/destination/golden-gate-park). You can download a free Official App to San Francisco Parks (appallicious.com/sf-rec-park). See what **special programs** might be offered in the park and the museums like:

Free Healthy Parks, Healthy People interpretive walks (10 a.m. the first Saturday of the month at Stow Lake at the Boathouse in Golden Gate Park).

Free Sunday afternoon Golden Gate Park Band concerts from April until October (at the Music Concourse in the park; goldengateparkband.org).

Free Saturday classes at the de Young and monthly artist-in-residence programs where artists design hands-on art-making activities.

Family Fun Days (the first and third Sunday of the month) with workshops, storytelling, and more at the Asian Art Museum. There are special live AsiaAlive performances.

Camp out overnight at the California Academy of Sciences through the Penguins and Pajamas Program.

Go behind the scenes to learn about the history of Steinhart Aquarium and how biologists care for the 38,000 animals—butterflies, fish, penguins, even an albino alligator—that live in the building.

Learn what coral reefs and rain forests have in common when you sign up for a special Adventure Tour and see what the California Academy of Sciences is doing to learn more about the creatures who live there.

WORD SEARCH: STAR LINGO

You can learn all about space and the scientists who study far off galaxies at the Morrison Planetarium at the California Academy of Sciences. Here are some useful terms to know if you're talking about stars:

- Astronomy is the study of space.

- The atom is the simplest building block of the universe.

- A comet is a small icy object from the outer part of the solar system.

- An extraterrestrial is any object, living or not, that originates from some place other than earth.

- An extremophile is an organism that has adapted to survive in extreme environments.

- A galaxy is a massive collection of stars and celestial objects bound together into a single system by gravity.

- A meteorite is a stony or metallic object from space that survives a fiery entry into the earth's atmosphere and lands on the surface.

- A solar system is a group of planets, moons, asteroids, comets, and other small objects that orbit one star.

Astronomy   Atom

Comet   Extraterrestrial

Extremophile   Galaxy

Meteorite   Solar system

```
T  A  E  I  N  G  G  S  S  B  V  M  S
A  L  X  B  V  T  O  N  O  E  U  E  O
B  L  T  M  R  G  A  L  A  X  Y  Q  L
M  X  R  T  H  Q  N  L  I  M  D  E  A
E  I  A  T  O  M  U  E  G  N  L  L  R
T  M  T  N  L  I  E  R  R  R  T  V  S
E  E  E  Q  L  E  C  S  T  O  K  E  Y
O  B  R  Z  C  O  M  E  T  N  S  R  S
R  R  R  Y  O  C  C  O  L  A  E  G  T
I  N  E  O  R  A  H  U  M  L  T  R  E
T  F  S  U  N  A  D  L  Y  N  C  W  M
E  X  T  R  E  M  O  P  H  I  L  E  U
E  C  R  Y  T  N  R  E  E  W  R  E  B
B  A  I  L  M  E  U  R  O  N  I  C  A
N  C  A  S  T  R  O  N  O  M  Y  L  Y
L  C  L  E  A  N  D  O  N  P  Q  Z  N
```

See page 149 for the answers

6

The Famous Bridge, Beaches & Marine Life

NO ONE GOT RICH BUILDING THE GOLDEN GATE BRIDGE

Many of the bridge builders worked for less than $1 a day. Their jobs were so high up that it took them more than half an hour to climb there. But they were glad for the work, though this was dangerous.

A huge trapeze-style net hung 60 feet below the men to catch them if they fell, but it didn't always work. Those who fell and survived called themselves the "Halfway to Hell Club."

Ready to walk across? Now you can really see how big it is. The main portion spans 4,200 feet over the water. The towers are as tall as a skyscraper!

Nothing says "San Francisco" to the world more than the Golden Gate Bridge, but at the time, a lot of people didn't want it built. They thought it would ruin the landscape!

DID YOU KNOW?

There are 80,000 miles of steel wire in the Golden Gate Bridge's two great cables, enough to circle the equator three times.

A part of the Golden Gate Bridge is always being painted. The orange color was originally chosen because it went well with the color of the sky.

The Golden Gate Bridge is 1.7 miles each way.

Bridge builder Joseph Strauss worked for 13 years, promoting the idea. Even after San Franciscans voted to build the bridge, it took 4 years and $35 million to build and opened in 1937. Today it would cost over a billion dollars.

Stop in at the **Golden Gate Bridge Pavilion.** It opened in time for the bridge's 75th anniversary and is the place to learn more about the bridge—and buy souvenirs.

On your way to the bridge, stop at **Fort Point** (nps.gov/fopo; 415-556-1693) just beneath the south tower of the bridge near the water's edge. It's a great place to get a close-up view of the bridge as well as to find out more about the Civil War soldiers who were stationed here when the fort was operational.

{ **What's Cool?** Biking across the Golden Gate Bridge.
You can rent bikes or sign on for an organized tour, like the ones offered at Bike and Roll (899 Columbus Ave.; 415-229-2000; bikethegoldengate.com).

You'll want to spend time in the **Presidio** near the bridge. It's a great place to explore with sandy beaches, rocky shore, woods, and lots of trails to hike and bike—all part of the Golden Gate National Recreation Area. Stop in at the Warming Hut that's both a place for a snack and a gift store. Take a walk along the Golden Gate Promenade. Kids especially like **Crissy Field** along the sand. It's actually marshland that has been restored, and you can skateboard, ride bikes, fly kites, or just play there.

Ready to build a giant sand castle?

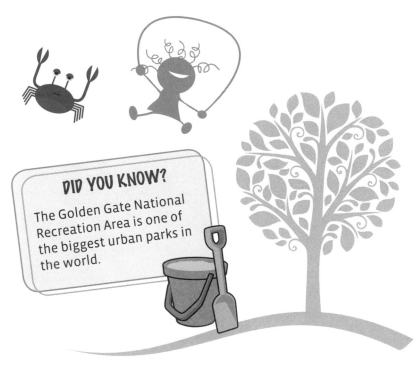

DID YOU KNOW?

The Golden Gate National Recreation Area is one of the biggest urban parks in the world.

Walt Disney—in San Francisco

Walt Disney got the idea for Disneyland from taking his daughters places. He thought there weren't enough opportunities for parents and kids to have fun together.

At the **Walt Disney Family Museum** in the Presidio with the Golden Gate Bridge in the background, you can see Walt Disney as a dad with hundreds of family pictures and find out how he imagined Disneyland before it was built—with a scale model. Watch the teacups spin! The downstairs theater shows free Disney movies (104 Montgomery St. off Lincoln Boulevard at the Presidio; 415-345-6800; waltdisney.org).

A LOCAL KID SAYS:
"My favorite museum is the Walt Disney Family Museum because I like learning about Walt Disney." —Anjali, 11

How You Can Help

The San Francisco Zoo hopes the animals who live here will inspire you to do what you can to protect animals who are in danger of disappearing.

Endangered species are those that are likely to become extinct. Many other species are *threatened,* which means that unless conservation efforts are started, they're likely to become endangered. Animals and humans are part of one world with one ocean, and it is up to us to protect them. Every day, you can do small, simple things to help the planet:

- Turn off lights when you leave a room.

- Turn off the television if no one is watching it.

- Create a recycling center in your home and recycle news-papers, glass, and aluminum cans.

- Turn off the water while brushing your teeth.

- Use both sides of a piece of paper.

- Plant wildflowers in your garden instead of picking them from the wild.

- Reduce the amount of trash you create and reuse your lunch bag each day.

- Don't buy animals or plants taken illegally from the wild or that are native to your area. Ask where they're from.

- Share what you know with your family and friends.

Grizzlies, Tigers & Gorillas

Ready to meet Kachina and Kiona? They're sisters who happen to be the resident grizzlies at the **San Francisco Zoo** (1 Zoo Rd.; 415-753-7080; sfzoo.org). You can watch them play in the water at Grizzly Gulch.

You might be able to help feed the lemurs at the zoo's Lemur Forest. These bug-eyed primates are from Madagascar.

> A LOCAL KID SAYS:
> "The monkeys are my favorite animals at the San Francisco Zoo because they are always screaming loud!"
> —Julia, 8

You'll also like the interactive exhibits at the **Primate Discovery Center.**

There are koalas and kangaroos, giraffes and zebras, kudus and ostriches, and a big **Children's Zoo** with its own insect zoo and lots of other animals.

Make sure to swing by the gorillas' home at the **Gorilla Preserve.** It's one of the biggest and most natural gorilla habitats of any zoo in the world.

Who is the funniest animal?

Bay Area Discovery

Want to help build your own Golden Gate Bridge? You can work on one just across the Golden Gate Bridge and within sight of its model in Sausalito at the **Bay Area Discovery Museum** (557 McReynolds Rd., Sausalito; 415-339-3900; baykidsmuseum.org) that's jammed full of indoor and outdoor activities for kids. It's on national park land in Fort Baker in nine restored buildings. Discover the habitat under the Golden Gate Bridge, explore a tide pool, or create a masterpiece in the Art Studio. You won't want to leave!

A VISITING KID SAYS:
"You are never too old to make sand castles!"
—Gabrielle, 13, Tucson, AZ

DID YOU KNOW?

The Golden Gate Bridge is orange, not gold. It got its name from the water that's underneath: The mile-wide Golden Gate channel is the entrance to San Francisco Bay from the Pacific Ocean.

Marine Mammal Health Care

Each patient gets lots of tender loving care as well as check-ups and medicines. But they get their pills served up inside raw fish. And these patients may weigh hundreds of pounds. Welcome to the **Marine Mammal Center** (2000 Bunker Rd., Sausalito; 415-289-7325; marinemammalcenter.org), a very special hospital where sick seals and sea lions as well as whales, dolphins, and porpoises are cared for. It's up on a hill in the Marin Headlands just north of the Golden Gate Bridge. They may have been bitten by sharks or cut on a boat propeller or have a disease that's made them weak. Some might be sick from eating garbage. There are new patients all of the time. Most survive and can return to the wild. The center staff takes care of them 24 hours a day just the way doctors and nurses would take care of you in the hospital. Come visit!

DID YOU KNOW?

Harbor seal pups can swim at birth but are almost always born on land. Mothers frequently leave them on the beach while they go look for food. Don't touch them or get too close if you see them.

TELL THE ADULTS:

Beaches are lots of fun, but they can also be dangerous, even if you aren't going in the water, like in San Francisco where the water is very cold. There are strong tides and waves! Drowning is the leading cause of accidental death for young children in California.

The American Red Cross has developed a free Swim App that provides parents and kids with water safety tips as well as games (redcross.org/mobile-apps/swim-app).

Designate an adult to be a "water watcher." Take turns even if there's a lifeguard on duty. Adults should be "touching distance" to preschoolers and toddlers around the water.

If kids are going in the water or playing at the shore, insist they are with a buddy.

Don't let kids swim unsupervised—even if there's a lifeguard on duty. Parents should watch younger brothers and sisters every second around the pool or ocean.

And when boating, even if everyone can swim, wear coast guard–approved life jackets.

CAN YOU FIND YOUR WAY TO THE GOLDEN GATE BRIDGE?

7
Dim Sum, Sushi &
Souvenirs

and you'll feel like you're in a different country.

There are brightly painted, pagoda-style buildings, red and gold streetlights, street signs in Chinese, and unusual foods in the store windows.

You'll notice all kinds of things in the shops that you've probably never seen before: whole roasted ducks and pigs, piles of sharks' fins and sea slugs, and big vats of jook, the creamy rice dish that the Chinese like to eat for breakfast.

Families come to **Chinatown** to shop as well as to eat. It's one of San Francisco's top tourist attractions (sanfran ciscochinatown.com). You'll see small, busy restaurants everywhere, upstairs and downstairs. Can you eat with chopsticks? Try them out on some Chinese noodle dishes.

Visit a tea shop. There are hundreds to choose from. The Chinese drink tea all day long. Sharing a cup of tea is a sign of respect and friendship.

The 24 blocks of Chinatown are narrow, crooked, and crowded. Thousands of Chinese immigrants and Chinese Americans live here. Many residents don't speak English. In fact, many of the older folks never venture outside Chinatown.

Start at **Portsmouth Square.** People call it Chinatown's living room. You'll see lots of Chinese seniors playing poker and Chinese chess. They come here every day. Grandmothers visit as they watch their grandchildren play on the swings.

Chinese workers have been coming to San Francisco since the gold rush. They ran laundries, opened clothing factories and restaurants, worked on the railroad, and settled in Chinatown.

DID YOU KNOW?

San Francisco's Chinatown is the largest Chinatown outside of Asia as well as the oldest Chinatown in North America. It is one of the top tourist attractions in San Francisco.

To learn more about Chinatown history, visit the **Chinese Historical Society of America** (chsa.org) on Clay Street.

Because there are so many people in San Francisco from so many places, it's a great place to shop and try different kinds of food. For example, walk just a few blocks north from Chinatown, and you're headed into the pizza and spaghetti land in **North Beach.** There are close to 100 Italian restaurants here! Go to **Japantown** for sushi and ramen noodles and to take a picture at Japantown's 100-foot-high Peace Pagoda. The Japanese have lived in this neighborhood since after the Great Earthquake of 1906. During World War II, when the US was at war with Japan, families were forced from their homes, but after the war, many returned.

For more shopping, you'll find department stores and the Westfield Mall in Union Square, souvenir stops along Fisherman's Wharf, and everything Giants and Raiders.

But you'll also find lots of things you won't find elsewhere—like every variety of origami paper in Japantown.

What origami animal are you going to make?

Dim Sum

In Chinese, *dim sum* means "point to the heart." Instead of looking at a menu, the food is wheeled around on carts. You point to what you want from the assortment of dumplings stuffed with a variety of fillings: shrimp and pork, vegetables, and beef. Act fast before the waiter or waitress whizzes by. People in San Francisco eat dim sum for lunch or brunch. It's delicious!

A LOCAL KID SAYS:
"Dim sum is one of my favorite foods. Everyone likes dim sum!"
—Andy, 14

Here's a guide to help you choose, courtesy of San Francisco Wok Wiz tours:

- *Cha sil bow*—steamed pork bun

- *Chern goon*—egg rolls

- *Jin dooey*—sesame-seed ball filled with lotus paste

- *No mi gai*—lotus leaf stuffed with sticky rice, chicken, pork, and shrimp

- *Lo bok go*—turnip cake

- *Gee bow gai*—paper-wrapped chicken

The Edible Schoolyard

It started as a way to clean up a school's grounds.

Now, nearly two decades later the Edible Schoolyard Berkeley (edibleschoolyard.org) grows more than 100 varieties of seasonal vegetables, herbs, vines, berries, flowers, and fruit trees, raises chickens that produce 500 eggs a year, and has become a model for teaching kids about healthy eating around the world. Many students say the time they spent in the Edible Schoolyard was what they remember most about middle school!

The Dining Commons at King Middle School now serves as the central kitchen for all 16 schools in Berkeley, providing wholesome, fresh, and mostly organic ingredients. The idea is to help kids see the connections from the garden to the kitchen and lunchroom.

Do you have an edible garden at your school? Maybe you could help start one!

Before You Go Souvenir Hunting

- Look for something that you can buy only in San Francisco—something with a cable car or the Golden Gate Bridge, for example.

- Consider if you want one big souvenir or several smaller things to add to a collection like pins, patches for your backpack, or stickers that you could put on your water bottle.

- Resist impulse buys.

DID YOU KNOW?

Each of San Francisco's neighborhoods has one-of-a-kind stores you won't find anywhere else.

What's Cool? Shopping for a kite at the Chinatown Kite Shop (717 Grant Ave.; 415-989-5182; chinatownkite.com).

Eating Smart on Vacation

Vacations are a good time to try different foods other than just what is on a kids' menu. That's especially true in San Francisco where you'll find every variety of food and plenty that is grown locally. Here's how you can eat healthier and try new foods:

- Split a portion of something with your brother or sister, or your mom or dad.

- If there is something you like on the grown-up menu, ask if you can get a half portion or order an appetizer size.

- Opt for fruit as a snack instead of chips or candy.

- Visit and talk to the farmers at the farmers' markets.

- Drink water rather than a soda. Your reusable bottle becomes a souvenir when you put stickers on it from all the places in San Francisco you've been!

DID YOU KNOW?

A Chinese doctor is always on hand at the Great China Herb Co. to tell you what herbs and teas will cure what ails you (857 Washington St.; 415-982-2195). This is a good place to buy tea too!

San Francisco is a great place to encourage kids to try new foods, whether with a picnic of goodies bought at a local farmers' market or a visit to an ethnic restaurant or upscale eatery that welcomes junior foodies. Don't be shy about asking if you can order a half or appetizer portion. Here are some places popular with kids and adults alike:

> A LOCAL KID SAYS:
> "I like to eat fortune cookies from the Fortune Cookie Factory in Chinatown."
> —Cash, 10

For the ultimate Chinatown experience try **Great Eastern** in Chinatown (649 Jackson St.; 415-986-2500; greateasternsf.com). Kids love the tanks filled with sea creatures.

For dim sum two options are **New Asia** in Chinatown (772 Pacific Ave.; 415-391-6666) or **Yank Sing** on the Embarcadero (1 Rincon Center; 415-781-1111; yanksing.com).

For sushi and house-made ramen noodles go to **Sapporo-ya** in Japantown (1581 Webster St., #202; 415-563-7400).

For Vietnamese food served family-style with great views visit **The Slanted Door** and sit outside overlooking the water (1 Ferry Building on the Embarcadero; 415-861-8032; slanteddoor.com).

For award-winning pizza in North Beach, you can't beat **Tony's Pizza Napoletana North Beach** (1570 Stockton St.; 415-835-9888; tonyspizzanapoletana.com). Or maybe you'd like homemade pasta where the chef sings at **Trattoria Pinocchio** (401 Columbus Ave.; 415-392-1472; trattoriapinocchio.com).

Tacolicious has three locations around San Francisco, including a Thursday Taco Stand at the Ferry Building Farmer's Market with innovative tacos (tacolicious.com).

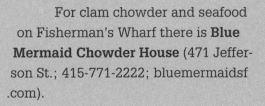

For clam chowder and seafood on Fisherman's Wharf there is **Blue Mermaid Chowder House** (471 Jefferson St.; 415-771-2222; bluemermaidsf.com).

If you are looking for breakfast downtown, **Sears Fine Food** is famous for its tiny pancakes (439 Powell St.; 415-986-0700).

For dinner with room to run around go to **Park Chalet Garden Restaurant** (parkchalet.com) right behind the famous **Beach Chalet** (beachchalet.com) at the edge of Golden Gate Park and with a well-priced kids' menu (1000 Great Hwy.; 415-386-8439).

For a kid-friendly breakfast, lunch, or dinner, **Park Chow** is known for organic chicken, burgers, mini pizzas, a kids' menu, and home-baked desserts (1240 9th Ave.; 415-665-9912; chowfoodbar.com).

For burgers, pull into one of the **Super Duper Burgers** all around the city (superdupersf.com).

For amazing pastries brave the lines out the door at **Tartine Bakery** (600 Guerrero St.; 415-487-2600; tartinebakery.com).

LEARN THE LANGUAGE!

Ni hao! That's how you say hello in Chinese (*tip:* It's pronounced like "knee-how") . . . but you won't often see it written down this way. That's because, unlike most languages you might be used to seeing, Chinese isn't written using the alphabet letters English speakers are used to. Instead, Chinese uses a set of characters. For example, this is what "hello" looks like in Chinese characters: 你好. Unlike letters, many Chinese characters represent more than just a sound; they can also be associated with objects or ideas! Ready to learn some more? Unscramble the letters next to each set of characters to find out what they mean!

旅游	LETRVA	Travle
家庭	MAILYF	Family
孩子	DLRCIHEN	children
探索	PLXOERE	Explore
食物	ODOF	Food
欢迎	MEWOELC	Velcome
谢谢	KTANH OYU	Thank you

Want to put your language skills to use? Here's how you pronounce the Chinese words and phrases you just unscrambled!

旅游 Lüyóu (loo-yo)
家庭 Jiatíng (jia-ting)
孩子 Háizi (hai-zuh)
探索 Tànsuo (tan-soo-oh)
食物 Shíwù (shih-woo)
欢迎 Huanyíng (huan-ying)
谢谢 Xièxiè (shee-shee)

See page 150 for the answers

A LOCAL KID SAYS:
"You should not leave San Francisco without getting noodles in Chinatown."
—Ries, 8

8

Buddhas, Gardens,
Cartoons & Modern Art

HISTORIC STAGECOACH, CARTOONS, OR MODERN ART?

Maybe you'd rather record a family memory or check out a real gold nugget.

You can do all that and more at San Francisco **museums** that welcome kids as much as grown-ups. San Francisco is a great place to visit a museum—or two! Go to a concert—maybe in the park! Or see a dance performance. You'll have your pick whenever you visit.

> A LOCAL KID SAYS:
> "I like the Asian Art Museum because of the dragon and animal paintings."
> —Adrian, 11

Museum shops can be good places to find interesting souvenirs and books for kids, especially if you liked a certain exhibit. San Franciscans love the Museum Store at the **San Francisco Museum of Modern Art.** While the museum is closed—it's being expanded—you can see some of its collection at other museums and stop in at the museum's temporary store (51 Yerba Buena Ln.; 415-357-4000; sfmoma.org).

You'll find several museums right downtown in the SOMA neighborhood:

The Contemporary Jewish Museum (736 Mission St.; 415-655-7800; thecjm.org) is always free for kids. Borrow a museum ART Pack that will help you understand the exhibits. There's one that will encourage you to share family memories. This is the museum where you can record those memories at the Story Corps Story Booth (thecjm.org/ on-view/in-the-past/story corps-storybooth) and another with a sketch- ing paper and pencils. Come for drop-in art- making workshops on Sunday!

DID YOU KNOW?

Gold rush miners set up their tents in the area of the city known as SOMA—which stands for South of Market Street. Today, there are fancy hotels, offices, apartments, and museums here.

The **Cartoon Art Museum** is the place to learn all about cartoons—and how to create them yourself (655 Mission St.; 415-227-8666; cartoonart.org). Check out Batman and other famous cartoon characters at the entrance!

The **Museum of the African Diaspora** explores the influence of people of African descent—from stories of the courage of slaves to art and music to the civil rights movement (685 Mission St.; 415-358-7200; moadsf.org). There are

DID YOU KNOW?

The US tried to buy Northern California from Mexico back in 1835. But Mexico refused and tried to sell California to England. California became part of the US in 1848 after the Mexican-American War.

special family tours and workshops with storytelling, crafts, and performances. You'll love the 3-story photo mosaic!

The **California Historical Society** is the place to learn all you want to know about the gold rush with pictures and letters from miners and others who raced to the goldfields (678 Mission St.; 415-357-1848; californiahistorical society.org).

If you're wondering where you can find that stagecoach and gold nugget, head to the **Wells Fargo History Museum** downtown. It's in Wells Fargo's headquarters where the bank has been since it started here in 1852 (420 Montgomery St.; 415-396-2619; wellsfargohistory.com).

Try the working telegraph!

A LOCAL KID SAYS:
"I like living in San Francisco because of all the diversity here."
—Joseph, 13

More Than a Garden

Smack in the middle of downtown, **Yerba Buena Gardens** are a place where you'll find spots to play, eat, and see art (750 Howard St.; yerbabuenagardens.org). It's a great place for a break if you're visiting the museums nearby or shopping or going to the movies at the huge **Metreon Mall** (135 4th St.; 415-369-6000; westfield.com/metreon).

All spring and summer—from May to October—there are special free performances and family programs during the **Yerba Buena Gardens Festival** (ybgfestival.org).

Join the fun!

A LOCAL KID SAYS:
"The Yerba Buena playground is big, and the slides are fun!"
—Emily, 11

In Front of or Behind the Camera

You can take your pick at the **Children's Creativity Museum.** You'll find it in the Yerba Buena Gardens complex near the ice rink. Take a ride on the Creativity Carousel outside (221 4th St.; 415-820-3320; creativity.org).

Inside, you can star in your own movie with creatures you make out of clay in the Claymation Studio or record a music video or your own symphony in the Music Studio. Dress up to get in character. Make your face look really funny with a computer program or play at the LEGO wall.

In the Design Studio, create an album cover for your music video or a poster for your movie. Stop in at the Innovation Lab and take the Mystery Box Challenge.

What can you invent—using just what's in the box?

{ **What's Cool?** Making a movie or a music video at the Children's Creativity Museum that you can take home and show your friends (221 4th St.; 415-820-3320; creativity.org).

TELL THE ADULTS:

San Francisco is a great place to go to a concert or a dance performance. There are **concerts and festivals** all during the year. Here's just a sample:

The **Hardly Strictly Bluegrass Festival** in Golden Gate Park, the city's top free music festival, is held in the fall (hardlystrictlybluegrass.com).

The **San Francisco Jazz Festival** is held around San Francisco in October (sfjazz.org).

The **San Francisco Symphony** hosts special family concerts (sfsymphony.org). Check out the website just for kids (sfkids.org).

The **Stern Grove Festival** has Sunday afternoon performances of symphony, opera, jazz, pop music, and dance in an outdoor amphitheater (Sloat Boulevard at 19th Avenue; 415-252-6252; sterngrove.org).

A cappella chorus **Chanticleer's** Christmas concerts are a San Francisco tradition; also check out the National Youth Choral Festival in early spring (415-252-8589; chanticleer.org).

Old First Concerts include a variety of music and vocal solos on Friday nights and Sunday afternoons (1751 Sacramento St.; 415-474-1608; oldfirstconcerts.org).

Smuin Ballet uses popular music in its performances (415-556-5000; smuinballet.org).

At **ODC,** families especially like the dance troupe's holiday offerings (351 Shotwell St.; 415-863-6606; odcdance.org).

Explore Asia

Ready to travel back in time thousands of years? You can at the **Asian Art Museum** in San Francisco (200 Larkin St.; 415-581-3500; asianart.org).

It has one of the largest collections of Asian Art outside of Asia and going back 6,000 years from all of the major cultures of Korea, Japan, China, India, Afghanistan, and more. Asia, of course, is not one place but many countries and cultures. This museum, which has a lot of family programs, is a good place to explore Asia with special family performances, hands-on art workshops, storytelling, and more. You can even try Asian food here—at Café Asia.

Start at the top and work your way down. See how Buddhism has influenced Asian civilization for more than 2,000 years. How many Buddhas do you see? Take a look at a Koran and the Chinese calligraphy and amazing brush paintings. Check out the puppets from Java.

There's too much here to see in one visit. You might want to focus on one country or culture.

Maybe it's time for a scavenger hunt. How many different animals can you find?

MAKE YOUR OWN MASTERPIECE

You've had the chance to explore the work of other artists—now it's your turn to get creative! Use the space below to draw your own original work of art!

9
Sea Otters, Whales, Butterflies & Roller Coasters

LOOK AT THEM GO!

The sea otters dive and tumble and play. You'll wish you could go swimming with them.

Watch them from below the water as they swim "upstairs" and then back down in their 2-story home at the **Monterey Bay Aquarium** (886 Cannery Row, Monterey; 831-648-4800; montereybayaquarium.org).

Get nose to nose up above. Check them out at mealtimes! Maybe you'd like to try some of that raw squid or abalone too.

The otters you see here were rescued as abandoned pups and hand-raised by the aquarium staff. They live in a protected home, but with the same plants and animals that wild otters encounter along the California coast.

DID YOU KNOW?

Fewer than one in 1,000 sea turtle eggs grow up to be adult turtles. To beat the odds, turtles lay thousands and thousands of eggs. You can help them by leaving their eggs alone.

What's Cool? Feeding the animals on a Behind-the-Scenes Tour at the Monterey Bay Aquarium before the aquarium opens to the public.

Look outside in the water for the harbor seals that swim here. Sometimes sea lions sun themselves on the rocks, barking at passing boats. In the winter, you may spot the gray whales as they swim south.

Inside the aquarium, check out the **Enchanted Kelp Forest.** It's 3 stories high! Here you can see the undersea world that thrives just outside in Monterey Bay. In the wild, some of the kelp plants are 100 feet tall! Hundreds of sea creatures call the kelp forest home. You can feel the kelp yourself and get a close-up look at its parts.

A LOCAL KID SAYS:
"I've learned a lot from tide pools about creatures I never knew about."
—Andi, 13

Wherever you wander in the huge Monterey Bay Aquarium, you'll get a new understanding of the world just outside in the bay and the ocean. The aquarium's researchers are working hard to learn more about them.

Check out the shapes and colors and sizes of the creatures—the delicate moon jellies and constantly changing octopuses, the frogs and turtles, the hermit crabs and anemones. Each is amazing to watch.

Reach out and touch the bat rays in the **Bat Ray Petting Pool** and then explore the touch pool.

Greet all the shorebirds at the **Sandy Shore Aviary** and see them really close up.

What's your favorite sea creature?

DID YOU KNOW?

Most migrating birds and whales travel the same route every year. But the tens of thousands of monarch butterflies that migrate to Pacific Grove every winter are too young to have ever been there before. The free Pacific Grove Museum of Natural History is a good place to find out more about them (165 Forest Ave., Pacific Grove; 831-648-5716; pgmuseum.org).

When you're ready to leave the aquarium, you can go on a fishing trip or board a whale watching ship from here. Explore the **Monterey Bay National Marine Sanctuary** by kayak or surfboard. Check out montereybay .noaa.gov to find out where you can rent surfboards or join a kayak tour.

In its heyday, boatloads of salmon, tuna, and sardines were unloaded here. Today, the old wooden wharf is home to all kinds of shops, outdoor fish markets, and restaurants that still use recipes handed down from the generations of anglers in families. Is it time for lunch yet?

Pick your own fruits and vegetables north of Monterey. There are kiwi and apples, raspberries, even pumpkins in the fall. Look for the signs for the farms.

If you're visiting in the fall or winter, you'll want to go to Pacific Grove (ci.pg.ca.us), dubbed **"Butterfly Town U.S.A.,"** to see the swarms of monarch butterflies. Pacific Grove is also home to **Point Pinos Lighthouse** (pointpinoslighthouse.org), California's oldest continuously operating one. Don't be concerned about finding the butterflies. There are thousands. They come here for the winter. You can't miss them.

Don't forget your wings.

A LOCAL KID SAYS:
"I love to go to tide pools. I like to see what's under me when I'm swimming or surfing. I also love going to the beach to play volleyball."
—Mara, 12

What's Cool? The celebration and Kids Parade every fall in Pacific Grove when the monarch butterflies arrive. Kids dress in butterfly costumes for the parade!

Whales

Look for the "blow."

When a whale comes up to breathe, it spews a cloud of air and water as high as 15 feet every 30-50 seconds.

Each winter, thousands of gray whales travel south from Alaska along California's coast to Baja, where they have their babies in the warmer water. They travel together in small groups fairly close to shore.

In spring, summer, and fall, you can see humpback whales, blue whales, and dolphins that migrate to central California waters each year to feed during summer and fall. Many whale watching trips are offered along the California coast, especially in Monterey. **Monterey Bay Whale Watch** offers trips all year led by a naturalist (84 Fisherman's Wharf, Monterey; 831-375-4658; gowhales.com).

Don't forget your binoculars.

Cannery Row

Fudge or ice cream? You'll find both on **Cannery Row** (555 Abrego St., Monterey; 831-649-6690; canneryrow.com) in Monterey, along with all kinds of souvenirs. As you browse, think about what it was like when fishermen and cannery workers were everywhere here. Slide down the tubes at the **Dennis the Menace Playground** (777 Pearl St., Monterey; 831-646-3860; monterey.org). Hank Ketcham, who created *Dennis the Menace,* designed the park.

Head out on the **Monterey Peninsula Recreation Trail** (mprpd.org) along the bay for a walk or a bike ride. Go to **Monterey Wharf** (montereywharf.com) to see if you can catch dinner.

Have any luck?

Tide Pools

They're rocky pockets by the shore that hold water in when the tide goes out. Some are large and others very small. They're home to an entire community of sea life—anemones, sponges, worms, snails, sea slugs, mussels, crabs, starfish, and sea urchins.

Hundreds of different creatures live here. Visit the **Seymour Marine Discovery Center** at Long Marine Laboratory in Santa Cruz (ucsc.edu/seymourcenter) to learn more about tide pools and the scientists who study them.

There are plenty of tide pools for you to explore too along the rocky coast at **Asilomar Beach** in Pacific Grove (ci.pg.ca.us) or at **Natural Bridges State Park** in Santa Cruz (2531 W. Cliff Dr., Santa Cruz; 831-423-4609; parks.ca.gov).

Low tide is the best time to explore. Look for hermit crabs, sea snails, stars, and anemones. If you're lucky, you might see an octopus.

Remember these sea creatures are fragile. Even turning over a rock can hurt a tiny animal not used to the sun. Don't take anything home!

Even empty seashells might provide a home for some animal later.

Santa Cruz

Plop yourself down on the sand on a Santa Cruz beach (santa cruz.com/Beaches) and build a gigantic sand castle.

Wave hi to the sea lions. You'll find them underneath the Municipal Wharf (ci.santa-cruz.ca.us/pr/wharf).

The **Boardwalk** is waiting for you when you're ready for some different fun in the sun (400 Beach St., Santa Cruz; 831-426-7433; beachboardwalk .com). Here's one National Historic Landmark your parents won't have to talk you

into touring. People have been coming here to play for 100 years, and kids like it just as much as they did at the beginning.

There's an arcade and miniature golf, plenty of food, and lots of rides. Don't miss the Giant Dipper wooden roller coaster. It's been here for more than 90 years and is still the Boardwalk's most popular ride.

Take a different ride aboard the **Roaring Camp & Big Trees Narrow Gauge Railroad** (roaringcamp.com) in nearby Felton through a redwood forest or down to the Boardwalk. It stops right in front of the carousel.

Can you catch a brass ring?

John Steinbeck

By the time he was a teenager growing up in Salinas, California, John Steinbeck was already scribbling stories and entertaining his friends with his storytelling. He grew up to become one of the most famous and popular authors in the US.

Steinbeck wrote about the lives of migrant laborers and cannery workers in Monterey, among other things. His novel *Cannery Row* is set in Monterey. You may know his story *The Red Pony*. His greatest novel, *The Grapes of Wrath,* told the story of the Joad family, who were driven off their Oklahoma land by the 1930s dust bowl and came to California.

Visit the **National Steinbeck Center** (1 S. Main St., Salinas; 831-796-3833; steinbeck.org) in Salinas. Take a literary walking tour through the town where Steinbeck grew up and see the school where he first learned to write.

DID YOU KNOW?

The male sea horse carries and births the young. The female puts her eggs in a pouch on his belly. Imagine a pregnant dad!

TELL THE ADULTS:

Even if it's cloudy, you've got to wear sunscreen. Doctors say there's a direct relationship between sunburns when you're young and skin cancer when you're grown. That's why if you're going to be outside you need sunscreen. Get one that provides all-day protection and that's waterproof.

Insist kids also get out of the sun every 90 minutes or so for a short break. And make sure everyone gets plenty to drink.

What you need: sunscreen that is considered "broad spectrum" and that has a sun protection factor, or SPF, of 15 and above. Broad spectrum is the new way to describe a sunscreen that blocks both types of damaging solar rays.

Reapply every 2 hours, according to the American Academy of Pediatrics, even on cloudy days and especially after the kids have been in the water.

WHAT'S THAT WORD?

Oceanographers use their own unique terminology to talk about creatures of the sea. See if you can match each word with its definition!

A) Flukes _____ A leap out of the water by an animal such as a dolphin, penguin, or sea lion.

B) Spyhop _____ When a whale, dolphin, or sea lion jumps out of the water and lands on its side or back.

C) Lobtail _____ The horizontal lobes of the tail of a whale, dolphin, or porpoise, made of connective tissue (not bone).

D) Bow _____ When the animals slap the tail flukes on the surface of the water.

E) Breach _____ To rise vertically out of the water so that the eye is above the surface.

See page 150 for the answers

10

Redwoods, Beaches &
Grapes

WHAT DOES A KID DO IN WINE COUNTRY?

Don't let the name of the region fool you, there are plenty of amazing things to see and do here! For one thing, you've probably never seen such big trees.

Welcome to the grove of towering redwoods at **Muir Woods National Monument** (1 Muir Woods Rd., Mill Valley; 415-388-2595; nps.gov/muwo). Here you're only 12 miles from the Golden Gate Bridge, but you'll feel like you're in another world.

And you *are* in a different world as you walk around some of the few remaining old-growth redwoods anywhere. These are all that's left of the redwood forests that once surrounded San Francisco Bay. We're lucky they're still here.

DID YOU KNOW?

Thousands of ladybugs cluster together at Muir Woods National Monument on horsetail ferns. It's an amazing sight!

What's Cool? Completing the Treasure Quest at Muir Woods National Monument. Download it before you go (nps.gov/muwo/forkids/upload/newMUWOquestWEB.pdf)!

Back in 1905, local couple William and Elizabeth Kent bought the land to protect one of the last stands of uncut redwoods and then donated 295 acres to the federal government to make sure it would always be kept safe. A few years later, when the area became a National Monument, they asked that it be named for California conservationist John Muir.

A LOCAL KID SAYS:
"At Muir Woods, I love going inside the huge trees and taking a photo!"
—Alexandra, 10

Did you know that coast redwoods are the tallest living things? And they're not only tall—some over 250 feet—but they're also wide. You won't be able to get your arms around the trunk!

You'll feel very small as you walk through **Cathedral Grove,** one of the most famous areas here.

Check out the big hollows in some of the trees—bigger than kids! Pioneers called them "goose-pens." In some redwoods they're so big that pioneers kept livestock in them.

Stop at the visitor's center and learn how you can become a junior ranger or go on a quest in the park and find hidden secrets with word clues in a poem.

See all the woodpecker holes in the trees?

Some of the trees here were already 500 years old when Christopher Columbus arrived in America.

A LOCAL KID SAYS:
"Going hiking and on my scooter are my favorite things to do outside."
—Mack, 8

Keep an eye out for wildlife along the way too. In the fall and winter on nice days, you might see some monarch butterflies. There are also black-tailed deer, chipmunks, ravens, snakes, lizards, wrens, and bright blue Steller's jays and northern spotted owls, though

DID YOU KNOW?

Silicon Valley is the nickname given to the area south of San Francisco where the computer industry got its start. Today companies like Google, Facebook, and many other start-up businesses are headquartered there.

they are tough to pick out with their natural camouflage and nocturnal habits.

If you want some beach time, just head from Muir Woods to **Muir Beach** (190 Pacific Way; nps.gov/goga) for a picnic or to **Stinson Beach,** where you can hike too. Local kids love Stinson Beach, and in winter Muir Beach Overlook is a good place to spot whales.

You won't want to miss the amazing beaches at **Point Reyes National Seashore** (75 Bear Valley Rd., Point Reyes Station; 415-464-5100; nps.gov/pore). There are special kids' programs at the Bear Valley Visitor Center.

Take a walk along the famous **San Andreas Fault** where the 1906 Great Earthquake started.

Bring a sweatshirt. It's going to be windy and cold, but perfect for beachcombing.

What did you find?

A VISITING KID SAYS:
"At a theme park, be brave and try everything because you don't know when you'll be back."
—Emily, 14, Phoenix, AZ

DID YOU KNOW?

Californians have been growing grapes for more than 150 years. Grapes are one of the state's top cash crops.

Coaster Thrills

Six Flags Discovery Kingdom is the place if you want to talk to the animals—from sharks to elephants to exotic birds to dolphins—and then ride a thrilling roller coaster or the Tsunami Soaker, about 30 miles north of San Francisco (1001 Fairgrounds Dr., Vallejo; 707-643-6722; sixflags.com/discoverykingdom). Feed a giraffe, swim with a dolphin, or ride an elephant during special encounters. See more than 500 butterflies flit around the trees as you walk through their habitat. Ready to ride the Boomerang Coast to Coaster?

California's Great America (4701 Great America Pkwy., Santa Clara; 408-988-1776; greatamerica.com) south of San Francisco in Santa Clara, has plenty of coaster action too, including the Gold Striker, which is the tallest and fastest wooden coaster lift in Northern California. Delirium features a powerful spinning pendulum that whirls you up high in the sky. Ride the Vortex stand-up coaster through all kinds of steel loops and twists. And there are water coasters. When you need a break, ride the world's tallest double-decker carousel, the Columbia Carousel.

Better wait for lunch until after the roller coasters!

Jack London

Before he was 30, Jack London was a world-famous author and reporter, even though he had dropped out of school as a young teen. Raised in Oakland, he'd gone to Alaska during the 1889 Alaskan gold rush, sailed the Pacific, and covered wars. London was one of the most popular authors of his day, and today kids and adults still enjoy his adventure stories like *Sea-Wolf, White Fang,* and *Call of the Wild.*

John Muir

John Muir began to speak out about the need to conserve the land and save the animals before anyone else did. Gradually, people began to listen—including President Theodore Roosevelt. Muir's efforts led to Yosemite becoming a national park in 1890. Two years later, he became the first president of the Sierra Club. In the Bay Area, he's considered a great hero. Muir Woods was named for him.

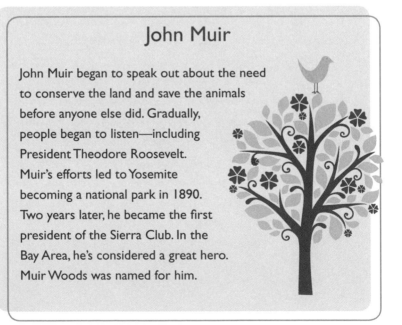

Berkeley

Want to see how your brain works? You can at the **Lawrence Hall of Science,** high on a hill on the University of California, Berkeley campus (1 Centennial Dr., Berkeley; 510-642-5132; lawrencehallofscience.org). This is another place that invites you in to see that science can be a lot of fun. Did you know you need to keep "exercising" your brain by using it?

The University of California, Berkeley is a huge school and a first-rate research destination. The city of Berkeley has always been known for its political protesters and freethinkers. You might see protesters here around Sproul Plaza.

Local kids like **Tilden Regional Park** with its carousel (ebparks.org/parks/tilden).

Before you leave, check out the street vendors on **Telegraph Avenue.** They sell all kinds of things you won't find in a mall—buttons and beaded jewelry and bumper stickers.

DID YOU KNOW?

Locals refer to the cities like Berkeley and Oakland across the San Francisco Bay as the "East Bay." When you cross the Golden Gate Bridge, you are heading north into Marin County.

TELL THE ADULTS:

Wine country isn't just for grown-ups, especially in Sonoma County, just north of San Francisco, where amid the wineries there's plenty for families to do:

View all kinds of exotic animals from a safari vehicle at the **Safari West Wildlife Preserve & African Tent Camp.** You can even camp here—just as you would in the Serengeti, listening to the animals (3115 Porter Creek Rd., Santa Rosa; 707-579-2551; safariwest.com).

Watch as millions of stickers get printed on a tour of **Mrs. Grossman's Sticker Factory,** the largest sticker company in the country. There's a sticker museum and of course the chance to buy plenty of stickers (3810 Cypress Dr., Petaluma; 800-429-4549; mrsgrossmans.com).

Visit a working farm where you might be able to go through a corn maze in fall, buy a Christmas tree at the holidays, sample fresh cheese, and maybe even see a baby lamb being born. Farmtrails.org has a map of farms that welcome visitors.

Take a horseback ride through a vineyard with **Triple Creek Horse Outfit** in Kenwood (2400 London Ranch Rd., Glen Ellen; 707-887-8700; triplecreekhorseoutfit.com) or along the beach at the **Chanslor Guest Ranch** (2660 Highway 1, Bodega Bay; 707-875-2721; chanslorranch.com).

Try your hand at cartooning at the **Charles M. Schulz Museum and Research Center.** Check out the 5-foot-tall painted statues of *Peanuts* characters in Santa Rosa (2301 Hardies Ln., Santa Rosa; 707-579-4452; schulzmuseum.org).

Take a hike or go on a bike ride in one of the many state parks (parks.ca.gov).

Check out the mini steam train that winds its way through 10 acres (2064 Broadway, Sonoma; 707 938 3912; traintown.com).

Visit the free outdoor sculpture garden at the **Paradise Ridge Winery** and stay for a picnic (4545 Thomas Lake Harris Dr., Santa Rosa; 707-528-9463; prwinery.com).

What's in Your Backpack?

When you're going hiking or to the beach, kids say you need:

- A reusable water bottle filled with water—two if you are going on a long hike! Put stickers on it and it becomes a souvenir.

- A rain jacket

- An extra layer in case you get cold

- Favorite snacks like trail mix you've made yourself

- A phone to take pictures (and keep in touch in case you get separated from your parents). Download apps like the Audubon Field Guides (audubonguides .com) that will help you identify flowers, birds, and trees along the way.

- A small magnifying glass to better explore what you are seeing along the trail

- Band-Aids

- Sunscreen: Use it even if it is cloudy!

WILDERNESS SLEUTH

You'll find more than just trees in the Muir Woods. This national park is teeming with wildlife! Listed below are some of the animals you might spy as you wander through. See if you can match each one to the correct set of tracks!

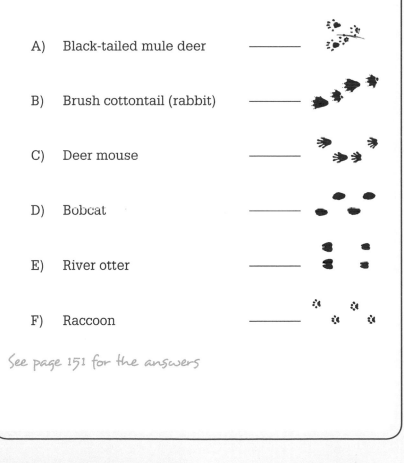

A)   Black-tailed mule deer   ———

B)   Brush cottontail (rabbit)   ———

C)   Deer mouse   ———

D)   Bobcat   ———

E)   River otter   ———

F)   Raccoon   ———

See page 151 for the answers

What a Trip!

I came to San Francisco with:

_____

_____

_____

The weather was:

_____

_____

_____

We went to:

_____

_____

_____

We ate:

_____

_____

_____

We bought:

_____

_____

_____

I saw these famous San Francisco sites:

_____
_____
_____

My favorite thing about San Francisco was:

_____
_____
_____

My best memory of San Francisco was:

_____
_____
_____

My favorite souvenir is:

_____
_____
_____
_____
_____
_____
_____

WHAT DID YOU SEE?

You had such a great time in San Francisco! Draw some pictures or paste in some photos of your trip!

Index

Answer Keys

Fill in the Missing Letters (p. 27)

UNION SQUARE

CHINATOWN

SOMA

NOB HILL

RUSSIAN HILL

NORTH BEACH

THE RICHMOND

THE SUNSET

THE HAIGHT

THE MISSION

Secret Word Decoder (p. 42)

Fisherman's Wharf

Word Search: Star Lingo (p. 71)

```
T  A  E  I  N  G  G  S  S  B  V  M  S
A  L  X  B  V  T  O  N  O  E  U  E  O
B  L  T  M  R  G  A  L  A  X  Y  Q  L
M  X  R  T  H  Q  N  L  I  M  D  E  A
E  I  A  T  O  M  U  E  G  N  L  L  R
T  M  T  N  L  I  E  R  R  R  T  V  S
E  E  E  U  L  E  C  S  T  O  K  E  Y
O  B  R  Z  C  O  M  E  T  N  S  R  S
R  R  R  Y  O  C  C  O  L  A  E  G  T
I  N  E  O  R  A  H  U  M  L  T  R  E
T  F  S  U  N  A  D  L  Y  N  C  W  M
E  X  T  R  E  M  O  P  H  I  L  E  U
E  C  R  Y  T  N  R  E  E  W  R  E  B
B  A  I  L  M  E  U  R  O  N  I  C  A
N  C  A  S  T  R  O  N  O  M  Y  L  Y
L  C  L  E  A  N  D  O  N  P  Q  Z  N
```

149

Learn the Language! (p. 96)

旅游 TRAVEL
家庭 FAMILY
孩子 CHILDREN
探索 EXPLORE
食物 FOOD
欢迎 WELCOME
谢谢 THANK YOU

What's That Word? (p. 123)

D A leap out of the water by an animal such as a dolphin, penguin, or sea lion.

E When a whale, dolphin, or sea lion jumps out of the water and lands on its side or back.

A The horizontal lobes of the tail of a whale, dolphin, or porpoise, made of connective tissue (not bone).

C When the animals slap the tail flukes on the surface of the water.

B To rise vertically out of the water so that the eye is above the surface.

Wilderness Sleuth (p. 137)

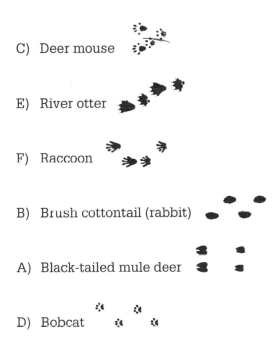

C) Deer mouse

E) River otter

F) Raccoon

B) Brush cottontail (rabbit)

A) Black-tailed mule deer

D) Bobcat

About the Author

Award-winning author Eileen Ogintz is a leading national family travel expert whose syndicated Taking the Kids is the most widely distributed column in the country on family travel. She has also created TakingtheKids.com, which helps families make the most of their vacations together. Ogintz is the author of eight family travel books and is often quoted in major publications such as *USA Today*, the *Wall Street Journal*, and the *New York Times*, as well as parenting and women's magazines on family travel. She has appeared on such television programs as *The Today Show*, *Good Morning America*, and *The Oprah Winfrey Show*, as well as dozens of local radio and television news programs. She has traveled around the world with her three children and others in the family, talking to traveling families wherever she goes. She is also the author of *The Kid's Guide to New York City*, *The Kid's Guide to Orlando*, *The Kid's Guide to Washington, DC*, *The Kid's Guide to Chicago*, *The Kid's Guide to Los Angeles*, *The Kid's Guide to Boston*, *The Kid's Guide to San Diego*, and *The Kid's Guide to Denver, Boulder & Colorado's Ski Country* (Globe Pequot).